Excel 2021

A Complete Guide to Master Excel 2021 Including All Its Functions, Formulae, and Additional Tips.

LANCE COLLINS

© Copyright 2021 by LANCE COLLINS- All rights reserved.

This document is geared towards providing exact and reliable information regarding the topic and issue covered. The publication is sold with the idea that the publisher is not required to render accounting, officially permitted, or otherwise, qualified services. If advice is necessary, legal or professional, a practiced individual in the profession should be ordered from a Declaration of Principles, which was accepted and approved equally by a Committee of the American Bar Association and a Committee of Publishers and Associations.

In no way is it legal to reproduce, duplicate, or transmit any part of this document in either electronic means or printed format. Recording of this publication is strictly prohibited, and any storage of this document is not allowed unless with written permission from the publisher. All rights reserved.

The information provided herein is stated to be truthful and consistent. In terms of inattention or otherwise, any liability, by any usage or abuse of any policies, processes, or directions contained within, is the solitary and utter responsibility of the recipient reader. Under no circumstances will any legal responsibility or blame be held against the publisher for reparation, damages, or monetary loss due to the information herein, either directly or indirectly.

Respective authors own all copyrights not held by the publisher.

The information herein is offered for informational purposes solely and is universal as such. The presentation of the information is without a contract or any guarantee assurance.

The trademarks used are without any consent, and the publication of the trademark is without permission or backing by the trademark owner. All trademarks and brands within this book are for clarifying purposes only and are owned by the book owners, not affiliated with this document.

Table of content

Introduction 10

Chapter 1: What is Excel? 13

1.1 How to open Microsoft Excel? 15
1.2 Understanding the Ribbon 15
1.3 Understanding the Worksheet 16
1.4 Windows Components for Microsoft Excel 17
1.5 Fill Handle 17
1.6 Quick Access Toolbar 18

Chapter 2: Learning MS Excel 2021 21

2.1 Creating a new workbook. 21
2.2 How to Enter Data? 21
2.3 Make the cell boundaries. 22
2.4 Custom Color palette 22
2.5 Draw and delete borders. 23
2.6 Change the color of your tabs 23
2.7 Fill the cell with remarks 23
2.8 Duplicate and copy the formatting 24
2.9 Identify any values that are duplicates 24
2.10 Create a hyperlink between a cell and a website 25
2.11 Include checkboxes in your design 25
2.12 Make a three-dimensional map 26

2.13 Apply cell shading 27

2.14 To add the data, use AutoSum 28

2.15 Create a basic formula. 28

2.16 Change the format of a number 29

2.17 Fill in the table with the data 29

2.18 Show totals for the numbers using Quick Analysis 30

2.19 A quick analysis to easily comprehend the results 31

2.20 Quick Analysis aids in the visualization of data in a table 31

2.21 Make a backup of the workbook 32

2.22 Make a copy of the workbook 32

2.23 Install and enable a plug-in 33

2.24 Locate and use a prototype 33

2.25 Freeze the Rows and Columns 34

2.26 Excel: Unlock Specific Cells 34

2.27 Authentication of data 35

2.28 Create a simple drop-down menu 36

2.29 To visualize results, use conditional formatting 37

2.30 Fill in the blanks 38

2.31 Used VBA to Make Macros 38

2.32 Proofing setting 39

2.33 Cell Formatting 40

2.34 Time and Dates 41

2.35 Styles 42

2.36 Cutting, Copying, and Pasting 43

2.37 Keeping Headings Visible 45

2.38 Adding a Row 46

2.39 Row resizing 46

2.40 Inserting a Column 47

2.41 Changing the Column Size 47

2.42 Shortcut menu 48

2.43 Formula Bar 48

2.44 Fill Handle 49

2.45 Fill data automatically in worksheet cells 50

2.46 Use of MS Excel spreadsheet 51

2.47 Some important shortcuts in MS excel 51

Chapter 3: Data Filling and Sorting 52

3.1 Data Sorting 52

3.2 Complex Sorts 54

3.3 Autofill 55

3.4 Autofill Dates 55

3.5 Autofill Numbers 55

3.6 Using Autofill for alternating text and numbers 56

3.7 Functions of Autofill 56

3.8 Filter the Data 57

3.9 How to delete Blank Rows 58

3.10 Protect Workbook 58
3.11 Make the Workbook Read-only 59
3.12 Make Meal Plan with Excel 60
3.13 Calculate your BMI with Excel 61

Chapter 4: Excel formulas and functions 64

4.1 What exactly is a formula? 64
4.2 Cell references 64
4.3 Absolute and relative references 65
4.4 Formulas may be copied and pasted 67
4.5 What is the best way to enter a formula? 67
4.6 How should you alter a formula? 68
4.7 Connecting Worksheets 68
4.8 What is a function? 69
4.9 Arguments of functions 70
4.10 How to enter a function? 71
4.11 Nesting (Combining Functions) 72
4.12 Math Operators 73
4.13 Logical operators 74
4.14 Order of operations 74
4.15 To convert formulas to values 75
4.16 Top 10 Basic Excel Functions 75
4.17 Excel Formulas 77
4.18 Use of AutoSum 78
4.19 Useful formulas for everyday activities 79

Chapter 5: Charts and Graphs 87

5.1 How to create a chart? 87
5.2 Chart Resizing..87
5.3 Moving a Chart.. 88
5.4 Moving chart elements....................................... 88
5.5 Formatting a Chart 89
5.6 Copying a Chart to Microsoft Word.................. 90
5.7 Incorporate a Graphic into a Chart................... 90
5.8 Change the Axis Scale 91

Chapter 6: XML to Excel Conversion 92

6.1 What is an XML file?...92
6.2 Excel XML File Import 93
6.3 Using the web URL, import an XML file into Excel 95

Chapter 7: Troubleshooting MS Excel 2021 ...97

7.1 Possible Reasons for not opening of MS Excel ..97
7.2 How to Open Excel Files That Won't Open 99
7.3 Uncheck the box that says "Ignore DDE". 99
7.4 How to turn off Ads-in 102
7.5 Microsoft Office can be repaired..................... 105
7.6 Excel File Associations Can Be Reset............... 108
7.7 Turning off Hardware Graphic Acceleration.... 111

Chapter 8: Applications of MS Excel 2021 ... 113

8.1 Financial and accounting uses 113

8.2 The Most Valuable Business Advantages of Microsoft Excel 114

8.3 What is the aim of Excel? 115

8.4 Excel's Employee Benefits...............................115

8.5 Making Improvements to The Skill Set 116

8.6 Improving The Data Organization 117

8.7 Productivity and Efficiency Enhancement 117

8.8 It Has the Potential to Make Your Job Easier... 118

8.9 How to Make Yourself a Valuable Employee at Work 119

8.10 It relieves the IT support team of stress 120

8.11 It allows you to make more use of an asset you already own.. 122

Conclusion 124

Introduction

Microsoft Excel is a spreadsheet-based software application that uses formulas and functions to arrange numbers and data. Excel analysis is utilized by companies of all types all around the world to do financial analysis.

Excel team aims to provide rich interactions for its customers in Excel for the web that improve productivity. They began improving the navigation and manipulation of Excel files in a browser, allowing the user to work in, and move through, a workbook and other connections faster and more fluidly. New functionality and capabilities today, including a new mini toolbar, table updates, and more, to help you quickly format your data with color and design are now launched.

The updated mini toolbar allows you to quickly access the most popular formatting commands by right-clicking.

For many Excel users, tables are second nature, and Excel wants to keep giving you a more clear table experience through desktop and mobile, from architecture and styling, to labelling, to total rows and more:

- Change the name of a table

- Add total rows
- All data may be formatted as a table

With the latest printing experience in Excel, which now supports print preview with page style settings, you can see what you're printing and configure it the way you like it:

Set the print area for the current collection, the active document, or the whole workbook.

Insert or remove Page breaks

Several situations, such as opening workbooks, navigating inside a workbook, and other encounters, have been discussed and changed. Take a look at the changes below:

Loading - The time required to load a workbook has been significantly shortened, making it easier for you to get started when operating with Excel for the internet.

Scrolling - Scrolling is an essential aspect of the Excel function. Scrolling is now smooth and easy, even in the most complicated sheets.

The need to engage with the material in your workbook is much more fundamental than scrolling. Cell selection pace, so you'll have less latency and a smoother experience while operating in the grid, has also been improved.

Navigating – Some navigation actions, including find/search, Go-To, and page-up and page-down, are now faster.

Changing – Excel made cell formatting and editing more effective.

After reading this book, you will understand the basic functions of MS Excel 2021, how to protect your workbook, and all the new features that are offered.

Chapter 1: What is Excel?

If you've worked in an office or been to school in the last 30 years, you're probably acquainted with Microsoft Excel. But, if you've been around longer, you're probably aware that it wasn't quite as common as its rivals.

"A programming product of such great importance or fame that it ensures the effectiveness of the technology for which it is associated," according to Merriam Webster. The PC of IBM and its broods were the most successful PCs of the 1980s, thanks to the success of Lotus 1-2-3, among other items. It comes as no surprise, then, that IBM bought Lotus Creation in the 1990s.

Microsoft Excel is a spreadsheet program for Windows, Android, macOS, and iOS that was created by Microsoft. It is a database application used primarily for recording and analysing numerical results. Consider a spreadsheet to be a table made up of columns and rows. Columns are normally allocated alphabetical characters, while rows are typically assigned numbers. A cell is the intersection of a column and a row.

As an example, all individuals work with numbers in some way. They all have regular bills that they compensate for from monthly earnings. To invest wisely, one must first understand their revenue and spending. When one needs to log, analyse, and store numeric details, Excel comes in handy.

Microsoft Excel is used in a variety of formats. It's available from a computer hardware store that also offers applications. Microsoft Excel is a software that is merely a fragment of the Microsoft Office suite. You can even get it from the Microsoft store, although you'll have to pay for the license key.

In today's complex business climate, custom solutions are required to maintain a competitive edge and optimize revenues. The most experienced in new and evolving developments are Microsoft Excel consultancy companies. Having a dedicated professional expert on retainer is vital to reaching the optimum strength and productivity required to excel in the twenty-first century. You can contact them right away, whether you need Excel solutions or preparation.

1.1 How to open Microsoft Excel?

Excel can be run in the same way as any other Windows application. If you're using a graphical user interface (GUI), such as Windows XP, Vista, or 7, follow the measures below:

1. Go to the Start menu.
2. Choose all programs.
3. Take your cursor to Microsoft Excel.
4. Click on Microsoft Excel.

1.2 Understanding the Ribbon

In Excel, the Ribbon gives shortcuts to different commands. An action taken by the user is a command. Printing a document, creating a new document, and so on are examples of commands.

Ribbon Start Button

The ribbon start button is used to execute commands such as generating new records, printing, saving existing writing, and having access to Excel's customization options, among others.

Ribbon tabs

These are used for group commands that are alike. Basic commands like editing data to render it more presentable, searching, and locating unique

data inside the spreadsheet are performed on the home page.

Ribbon bar

These bars are used to group commands that are identical. For example, to organize all of the actions that are applied for aligning data together is used.

1.3 Understanding the Worksheet

A worksheet is a collection of columns and rows. A cell is formed when a column and a row intersect. Data is recorded in cells. A cell address is used to identify each cell individually. Letters are used to mark columns, and numbers are used to label rows.

A list of worksheets is referred to as a workbook. A workbook in Excel comprises three sheets to begin with. To meet your needs, you can erase or add more sheets. Sheet1, Sheet2, and so on are the default names for the spreadsheets. You should rename them to something more important, like Daily Expenses or Monthly Budget.

1.4 Windows Components for Microsoft Excel

It's important to know where everything is in the window when you start using Microsoft Excel. So, ahead, are all the big components that you should be aware of before diving into the realm of Microsoft Excel.

A cell that is selected is known as an active cell. A rectangular box will be used to illustrate it, and its whereabouts will be displayed in the address bar. Clicking on a cell or using your arrow keys can activate it. You can double-click on a cell or use F2 to edit it.

A column is a vertical grouping of cells. A single worksheet may have up to 16384 columns. From A to XFD, each column will have a unique letter for identification. By clicking on a column's header, you can select it.

A row is a horizontal grouping of cells. A single worksheet may have up to 1048576 rows. For identification, each row has a unique number ranging from 1 to 1048576. By pressing the row number on the left side of the browser, you can select it.

1.5 Fill Handle

This is a tiny dot in the active cell's lower right corner. It helps you with inserting numeric values, text sequences, ranges, and serial numbers, among other things. The Address Bar displays the active cell's address. If you pick more than one cell, the first cell's address in the range will be shown. Below the Ribbon is the formula bar, which is an input bar. It displays the contents of the selected cell and allows you to type a formula into a cell.

The name of your workbook would appear in the title bar, accompanied by the program name ("Microsoft Excel"). The file menu, like many other programs, is a plain menu. It has choices such as Open, Save, Print, Save As, Excel Options, New, Share.

1.6 Quick Access Toolbar

A toolbar that allows you to easily analyze the actions you use the most. By clicking new options to the "quick access toolbar," you can add your favorite options.

Ribbon Tab

Beginning with Microsoft Excel 2007, all choice menus have been replaced by ribbons. Ribbon tabs are a set of various command groups that include additional options.

Worksheet Column

This tab displays all the worksheets in the workbook. Sheet1, Sheet2, and Sheet3 are the names of the three worksheets that will appear in your latest workbook, respectively.

Status Bar

At the base of the Excel pane, there is a thin bar. When you begin using Excel, it will be of immediate assistance.

You will build a toolbar in Excel that contains the commands you need the most. The Easy Access Toolbar helps you to quickly and efficiently complete your most common tasks.

1. Choose the File tab from the top left corner of your browser.

2. Choose Excel Options from the dropdown menu. This will bring up the Excel Options dialogue window.

3. Choose Customize from the left sidebar. The customization choices for your Quick Access Toolbar will appear.

To add a function to your toolbar, follow the steps below:

1. Choose a command from the left-hand scrolling menu.

2. Choose Include. The command has now been added to the right-hand list. The up or down arrows on the side of the browser may be used to reorder the commands on the toolbar.

3. Under the Ribbon box, choose Show Quick Access Toolbar.

4. Choose OK. The Quick Access Toolbar will now show below the Ribbon.

Chapter 2: Learning MS Excel 2021

Excel is an excellent medium for making sense of vast amounts of details. However, it's also useful for doing simple calculations and keeping a record of virtually every kind of reporting. The key to unlocking all the commitments is to use the matrix of cells. In cells, you'll find text, numbers, and calculations. Data is inserted into cells and then organized into columns and rows. It assists you in gathering information, arranging and filtering it, organizing it into tables, and creating visually pleasing charts. To get you started, let's go through the basics.

2.1 Creating a new workbook.

Excel documents are referred to as workbooks. Each workbook contains sheets, also described as spreadsheets. You can add as many sheets to a workbook as you like to keep the details seperate, or you can create new workbooks. Choose New from the File menu. From the New menu, select the Blank workbook option.

2.2 How to Enter Data?

By clicking on an empty cell, you actively select it. Cell A1 on a new sheet, for example. To apply them, the location of cells in the row and column on the sheet is used. As a result, cell A1 will be in the "A" column and "1" row. Insert either text or a number in the cell. Click Enter or Tab to move to the next cell.

2.3 Make the cell boundaries.

Choose a cell or a group of cells on a worksheet for which you want to add a boundary, change the border style, or exclude a border.

Select the cell (or cells) on which a boundary should be applied. To quickly pick the entire worksheet, press the Select All tab.

Pick the border style you like by clicking the down arrow beside the Borders Button icon in the Font tab on the Home screen.

2.4 Custom Color palette

Custom color palettes will help you match your brand colors or fine-tune your color choices:

By dragging the color slider in the more colors dialogue window, you can choose from a broad variety of color options.

Drag your mouse around the more colors rectangle to change the color hue, then check your pick in the preview box.

For fast color selection, enter RGB or hex values directly.

Apply cell types like number formats, fonts, and cell boundaries, and coloring to keep the styling of the Data clear, so it's simple to read and understand.

2.5 Draw and delete borders.

Through inserting or deleting cell boundaries, you may highlight the data or distinguish one collection of data from another. Choose Draw Border to create outer boundaries, Draw Border Grid to create gridlines, or Delete Borders to remove them entirely.

2.6 Change the color of your tabs

Suppose you have a lot of different pages in one document—which can happen to anyone—color-code the tabs to make it simpler to find where you need to go. You could, for example, color code last month's sales reports red and the current month's orange.

Simply right-click a tab and pick "Tab Color" from the context menu. A popup will open, allowing you to pick a color from an existing theme or design one to suit your requirements.

2.7 Fill the cell with remarks

When you want to write a note or add a remark to a particular cell in a worksheet, just right-click the cell and choose Insert Comment from the menu. To save your comment, type it into the text area and then click outside the comment area.

A little red triangle appears in the corner of cells that contain comments. Hover over the remark to see it.

2.8 Duplicate and copy the formatting

If you've ever spent time formatting a sheet to your satisfaction, you'll agree that it's not the most pleasurable experience. It's really rather tiresome.

As a result, you're unlikely to want to—or need to—repeat the procedure the following time. You can simply replicate the formatting from one region of a worksheet to another with Excel's Format Painter.

Pick the formatting you want to duplicate, then go to the dashboard and select the Format Painter option (the paintbrush icon). The cursor will turn into a paintbrush, asking you to pick the cell, text, or full worksheet to which you wish to apply the formatting.

2.9 Identify any values that are duplicates

Duplicate values, like duplicate content when it comes to SEO, may be problematic if left unchecked. However, in certain circumstances, all you need to do is be aware of it.

Whatever the circumstance, it's simple to find any existing repeating groups in your spreadsheet by following a few simple steps. To do so, pick Highlight Cell Rules > Duplicate Values from the Conditional Formatting menu.

Create a formatting rule to describe the sort of duplicate material you want to bring forth using the popup.

2.10 Create a hyperlink between a cell and a website

When utilizing sheets to monitor website analytics or social media, having a reference column alongside the links monitored by each row might be helpful. If you directly input an URL into Excel, it should automatically click it; but, if you need to hyperlink words, such as a title page or a post's headline, here's how to accomplish it.

Press Shift K after you've typed your linked terms. Set the tone with your remarks. From there, a box appears where you may enter the linked URL. Copy, paste, then press Enter. In this directory, type the URL.

2.11 Include checkboxes in your design

If you're using an Excel sheet to track customer information and want to track something that isn't measurable, you may add checkboxes to a column.

Whether you're using an Excel sheet to handle your clients' sales prospects and want to see if you called these cells in the previous trimester, you may have the column and check the cells in it when the customer is called.

This is how you can accomplish it with Excel 2021.

Choose a cell to which you'd want to add checkboxes and double-click it. Then choose Developer from the drop-down menu. Under "FORM CONTROLS," click the checkbox.

Once the box has appeared in the cell, copy and paste it into the cells where it will also appear.

If the primary shortcut does not function for whatever reason, you may do it manually by going to Insert>Hyperlink.

2.12 Make a three-dimensional map

Before Excel 2016, Power Map was a well-known free 3D geographical visualization add-in for Excel. It's now called 3D Maps, and is included in Excel for Office 365 for free. It may be used to plot geographical and other data on a three-dimensional globe or map. First, you'll need data that is suitable for mapping; then, you'll have to prepare it for 3D Maps.

While such measures are outside the scope of this book, Microsoft does provide guidance on how to gather and handle data for 3D Maps. After you've correctly prepared your data, open the spreadsheet and click Insert, then 3D Map, then Open 3D Maps. Then, in the popup window, choose Enable. This turns on the 3D Maps feature. For additional information on how to deal with the data and personalize your Display, see the Microsoft instruction "Get started with 3D Maps".

If you don't have any data for mapping but would like to see what a 3D map looks like, you may use Microsoft's example data. The picture above is from a Microsoft presentation for Dallas Utilities called Seasonal Electricity Consumption Simulation. After you've downloaded the workbook, go to Insert > 3D Map > Open 3D Maps, and then press the map to start it.

3D Maps may be used to plot geospatial data in an interactive 3D chart.

2.13 Apply cell shading

A single cell or a number of cells may have cell shading added to them. Choose the color you like under Theme Color, including Standard Colors, by clicking the arrow next to the Fill Color Icon in the Font group on the Home screen.

2.14 To add the data, use AutoSum

You will want to calculate the results you've entered into your spreadsheet. This can be done quickly by using AutoSum. Select a cell to the right of the amount you want to alter. Select the Home page, then the Editing team, and finally AutoSum from the drop-down menu.

2.15 Create a basic formula.

Excel is capable of more than adding numbers; it may also do various kinds of calculations.

- Use several simple formulas to bind, subtract, multiply, or divide quantities.
- Write the equal sign (=) in a cell that you've chosen.
- It alerts Excel that such a cell contains a formula.
- To construct a series of numbers and measuring operators, simply use the (+) plus sign for inclusion, the (-) minus sign for subtraction, the (*) asterisk sign for multiplication, and the (/) forward slash sign for division. As an example, enter =6-3, =13+2, =11*5, or =6/2.
- Press the Enter key on your keyboard. It brings the computation to a close.

You may also hold down CTRL and enter to keep the cursor on the active cell.

2.16 Change the format of a number

To distinguish between different types of numbers, use formats such as currencies, times, or percentages.

- Choose the cells that hold the numbers you want to format.
- After pressing the Home button, choose the arrow in the General box.
- Use the number format you want.

2.17 Fill in the table with the data

Inserting details into a table is a simple way to take advantage of Excel's capabilities. It is an efficient way of sorting and filtering your data.

- To pick a cell, click the first cell in the data and pass it through the last cell.
- When choosing data with the arrow keys, press and hold Shift on the keyboard.
- Press the Quick Access tab in the lower-right corner of a range.

- Choose a table, then move your cursor across the Table icon to see the details before pressing it.

- Press the Filter drop-down arrow in the column header. To filter the data, uncheck the Select Everything checkmark, then press the Data you want to view in your chart.

- To filter the data, choose Sort Z to A and Sort A to Z.

- Choose OK.

2.18 Show totals for the numbers using Quick Analysis

With the Quick Analysis function, you can quickly add up the numbers. If you choose average, count, or sum, Excel shows the calculation results under and next to the numbers. Select the cells you want to work with. Click the Quick Analysis tab in the bottom right of a selection. Also include numbers you choose to add or count.

Pick Totals, move your mouse over the keys, and then pick the button to add the totals and show the calculation results with your files.

2.19 A quick analysis to easily comprehend the results

Sparklines and conditional formatting can help you visualize important information and expose trends in your data. Use the Quick Analysis tool to get a live preview.

- Choose the information you want to investigate further.
- Press the Quick Analysis tab in the bottom-right corner of a range.
- Look at the Formatting and Sparklines tabs to see if they affect the files.

For instance, Choose a color code in the Formatting folder to differentiate between medium, moderate, and low temperatures. When you've found what you're searching for, press the mouse button.

2.20 Quick Analysis aids in the visualization of data in a table

The Quick Analysis tool (available only in Microsoft Excel 2013 and 2016) recommends the appropriate chart for the data and generates a visual view in a matter of seconds.

- Just choose cells in which the data for your chart would be processed.
- Press the Quick Analysis tab in the bottom-right corner of a range.
- Go to the Charts page, browse through the recommended charts, and choose the one that best matches your data collection.

2.21 Make a backup of the workbook

- On a Quick Access Toolbar, click Ctrl+S or the Save key.
- Whether or not you are saving this file for the first time, this way you've already saved the work.
- Under Save As, choose a place for the workbook to be saved and then browse to a folder.
- In the name box, give your workbook a name.
- Click the Save button.

2.22 Make a copy of the workbook

- Select File, then Print, or press Ctrl+P.
- Use the Next Page and Previous Page arrows to preview a page.

- The preview window displays a page in white and black color, depending on the printer settings.
- If you really don't like the page print, you can change the page margins or add page breaks.
- Choose Print.

2.23 Install and enable a plug-in

- From the File tab, choose Options, then the Add-Ins category.
- Choose Excel Add-ins in the Manage box in the lower left corner of the Excel Options dialogue box, then press Go.
- In the Add-Ins discussion pane, choose the checkboxes for the add-ins you want to use, then click OK.
- If Excel prompts you to install the add-ins after telling you that it can't, choose Yes to install them.

2.24 Locate and use a prototype

Excel allows you to use built-in models, build new templates, and search via an Office.com template library. It includes budget templates as well as a wide range of different Excel models.

2.25 Freeze the Rows and Columns

By scrolling through large datasets in a worksheet, you'll be able to pass data from the page. If you would like specific data to stay on the screen at all times, like column and row headings, you can freeze a section of the list so that it remains on the screen while the rest of the data scrolls.

Press in a cell to choose it, and go to the View tab and click the Window group, then Freeze Panes to freeze columns and rows. Excel can show black vertical and horizontal lines.

2.26 Excel: Unlock Specific Cells

There is an option to open individual cells in the Excel workbook. The whole workbook will be unprotected when you first start. After that, you can make whatever changes you like to the cells you would like to be secured. When you protect a worksheet, no one else can change it.

To protect your worksheet, choose Cover Worksheet from the Review tab. After you select this option, the Protect Sheet screen will appear. You'll then pick the tools you like to use to cover the frozen columns and rows.

- From the drop-down menu, choose Data >> Data Validation.

- Choose a list from the Allow package. Then type the options into the source box, separating them with a comma. Select a group of cells comprising the list elements as an alternative.

You will have a drop-down screen to help you enter data quickly and easily.

2.29 To visualize results, use conditional formatting

Conditional formatting is a widely used function of Excel. It enables the user to easily understand the details they're looking at. You'll use simple parameters to format cells automatically if a target is reached, a deadline has passed, or earnings have sunk below a certain level. As an example, the cell color should be modified to green if the input is greater than 300.

- Decide which cells should have Conditional Formatting added to them.

- Choose the Home page, then Conditional Formatting, Highlight Cells Rules, and Finally, Greater Than.

- Type 300 and then select the desired file.

While this example uses a green fill and font color, there are several formatting options available. Data bars and symbol sets may also be used for conditional formatting. These visuals have the ability to be extremely effective.

2.30 Fill in the blanks

Flash Fill is a wonderful function that makes it simple to change results. This role would significantly reduce the time required to execute repetitive data cleaning tasks that historically involved the use of formulas and macros. The names in column A collection are what you're looking for.

Fill in the first and second names in cells B6 and B3, and type as you proceed. Flash Fill notices a pattern in your acts and asks if you want it repeated throughout the rest of the rows. It's fantastic. The data will be retrieved until you click Enter. Flash Fill can be used in a number of different ways. The Data tab also has a Ctrl + E icon that can be reached by pressing Ctrl + E.

2.31 Used VBA to Make Macros

By using macros to automate repetitive tasks, you can increase your performance. These operations may seem complex, but they are, for the most part, simple tasks that are carried out on a regular basis. Macros help you accomplish activities faster and more regularly. You'll start by videotaping yourself performing Excel tasks to learn how to use macros. It will produce VBA JavaScript and a macro. On the View page, you'll find the macro recorder. It's the very last one.

You and your colleagues can save a lot of time by using macro capturing. If you want to take it a bit further, you may learn Excel VBA and customize your macros. You can use VBA to enable macros to do more than just report data and to create functionality that Excel lacks. To see the VBA code given by the recording, go to View >> Macros, select the macro from the chart, and press Edit.

2.32 Proofing setting

This option modifies the text that was previously entered into Excel. It allows you to configure features such as the dictionary terminology to be used while looking for misspellings, dictionary tips, and so on. This alternative is available under the proofing tab in the options dialogue window on the left hand side column.

Making Changes to a Worksheet.

Connect data to a cell; rotate across cells; add columns and rows to a spreadsheet; cut, duplicate, and paste cells; and resize rows and columns are all covered in this chapter. It also demonstrates how to use the freeze panes function, which helps you freeze column and row headings to make navigating a big worksheet easier.

2.33 Cell Formatting

From the Format Cells dialogue box, you can access formatting choices for cells.

Choose the cell you would like to format from the drop-down menu. Right-click the cell on a PC. Users on Macs can hold down Control and select the cell. Select Format Cells from the shortcut menu.

Click the arrow in the Number group on the Home page.

Formatting cells is done using the Format Cells dialogue box, which has the following options:

- Number tab – specifies the numerical data form, such as dollar, date, or percentage.
- Alignment tab – helps you move and coordinate data inside a cell.
- Font tab – helps you modify cell font attributes such as font face, height, type, and color.
- Border – enables you choose a border theme for your cell from a number of choices.
- Fill – helps you shade and paint the backdrop of a cell.

- Cell protection – the ability to secure or shield a cell.

2.34 Time and Dates

Excel inserts dates into a spreadsheet in the format 1-Jan-01 by default. Excel would immediately accept the text as a date and update it to "1-Jan-01" even if you type the date as "January 1, 2001." If you choose to use a different date format, follow these steps:

1. Select the cell in which you choose to apply the latest date format.

2. Choose the Home tab from the drop-down menu.

3. Choose the Format from the Cells community.

4. Select Format Cells from the drop-down menu. This will bring up the Format Cells dialogue box.

5. Choose the Number tab from the drop-down menu.

6. Choose a date from the Category menu.

7. From the drop-down menu, choose the date type you prefer.

8. Choose OK.

In addition, Excel joins periods in a particular manner. If you choose to use a particular time format, repeat the steps above but change the Category menu to time.

2.35 Styles

Excel has a range of pre-defined styles that you can use to quickly and conveniently format your worksheet. The various types even contribute to a professional and coherent appearance for your spreadsheet.

To apply a preset style to a cell or a group of cells in your worksheet, follow these steps:

1. To pick a cell, click it.

2. Choose the Home tab from the drop-down menu.

3. Choose Format as Table from the Styles community. A menu appears, displaying the various cell types. Keep the cursor over the menu choice to see a glimpse of a theme.

4. Click on the style you would like to use.

To apply a preset style to the whole worksheet, follow these steps:

1. Press CTRL + A on your keyboard to choose all the cells in your worksheet.

2. Choose the Home tab from the drop-down menu.

3. Choose Format as Table from the Styles community. A menu appears, displaying the formatting choices available. Keep the cursor over a menu choice to see a glimpse of a theme.

4. Click on the style you would like to use.

If you've formatted a cell with a certain font type, date format, border, or other formatting choices, you can use the Format Painter method to format another cell or group of cells in the same way.

1. Place your cursor within the cell wherever you want to copy the format.

2. Choose Format Painter from the Home page. Your mouse will now be accompanied by a paintbrush.

3. Choose the cells you would like to format from the drop-down menu.

Double-click the Format Painter button to copy the formatting to several groups of cells. When you click the buttons, the format painter will remain working.

2.36 Cutting, Copying, and Pasting

To switch cells from one position on a worksheet to another, first, cut or copy the cell(s), then paste the cell(s) in their new location.

To cut a cell, do the following:

1. To select a cell, click it.

2. Choose the Home tab from the drop-down menu.

3. Press Ctrl + X on your keyboard, or click the Cut button in the Clipboard group.

The cell should be surrounded by a flickering dotted border.

To duplicate a cell, follow these steps:

1. To select a cell, click it.

2. Choose the Home tab from the drop-down menu.

3. Press Ctrl + C on your keyboard, or click the Copy button in the Clipboard group.

The cell should be surrounded by a flickering dotted border.

To paste a cut as well as a copied cell to a different position on your worksheet, follow these steps:

1. To find a new position on your worksheet, click it.

2. Choose the Home tab from the drop-down menu.

3. Press Ctrl + V on your keyboard, or click the Paste button in the Clipboard group.

If you're only transferring the contents of a single cell a short distance, the drag-and-drop process could be more convenient.

1. Choose the cell you would like to move by clicking it. The cell's edges should be surrounded by a black border.

2. Drag the cell to its new position by clicking and dragging the cell's black line.

2.37 Keeping Headings Visible

If you have a large worksheet with a lot of row and column headings, they can vanish when you scroll down. You should use the Freeze Panes option if you want the headings to stay clear at all times. Separately freezing the column as well as row headings can be necessary.

To keep the row headings frozen, follow these steps:

1. On the left side of the worksheet, click the Row 1 heading.

2. Choose View from the drop-down menu.

3. In the Window group, click the Freeze Panes icon.

4. Choose Freeze Top Row from the menu.

To keep the column headings frozen, follow these steps:

1. At the top of the worksheet, click the column A heading.

2. Choose View from the drop-down menu.

3. In the Window group, click the Freeze Panes icon.

4. Choose Freeze First Column from the drop-down menu.

To unfreeze a panel, go to the View tab and press the Freeze Panes icon, then Unfreeze Pane.

Moving to a Particular Cell

To get to a particular cell:

1. Type the address of that cell address (letter followed by the number of the cell) in the address Box.

2. On the keyboard, press Enter.

2.38 Adding a Row

A row is a horizontal line that extends through a worksheet. To add a row in a worksheet, do the following:

1. Choose the worksheet on which you want the row to show.

2. Choose the Home tab from the drop-down menu.

3. In the Cells set, click the arrow on the Insert button.

4. Select Insert the Sheet Row from the drop-down menu.

Note: Doing so places a row above the currently selected cell.

2.39 Row resizing

To resize a row, do the following:

1. Pick the worksheet by clicking on it.

2. Move the cursor along the row heading's border until it switches to a plus symbol.

3. Drag the width of the row until you're comfortable with it.

Pick the row headings you wish to alter, then press and drag one of the rows to the correct distance.

2.40 Inserting a Column

A column is a vertical row that runs down a worksheet. To add a column, follow these steps:

1. Choose the worksheet on which you want the column to show.

2. Choose the Home tab from the drop-down menu.

3. In the Cells set, click the arrow on the Insert button.

4. Insert the Sheet Column from the drop-down menu.

Note: Doing so adds a column to the left of the currently selected cell.

2.41 Changing the Column Size

To resize a column, do the following:

1. Pick the worksheet by clicking on it.

2. Move the cursor along the column heading's border until it switches to a plus symbol.

3. Click and drag the column width until you're comfortable with it.

Select the column headings you wish to alter, then press and drag one of the columns to the correct distance.

2.42 Shortcut menu

To use the shortcut menu to insert rows or columns, follow these steps:

1. To add a new row or column, click the column letter or row number where you want it to appear.

2. If you're using a PC, right-click the column letter or row number; if you're using a Mac, control-click the row number/column label. A menu with shortcuts should appear.

3. From the shortcut menu, choose Insert.

- Rows: If you do this, the row would be added above the one you picked.
- Columns: If you do this, the column would be added to the left of the one you chose.

2.43 Formula Bar

As you progressively use Excel, this would be one of the most valuable methods. The formula bar displays all the information and procedures that were used to return the contents of a cell. When you enter data into a cell, the performance, or final outcome, is shown when you click away from the cell. This is particularly noticeable when utilizing functions since you only see the outcome of the equation in the cell in the worksheet, not the whole equation. The formula bar is underneath the Ribbon, which takes up most of the window.

While hiding the formula bar is feasible, it is not advised. Go to Excel Options at the lower corner of the menu that appears when you press the Office button to remove or reveal the formula bar if it has been obscured by accident. To see the formula bar, go to the advanced alternative and check the box for the Show formula bar under Display. Simply press OK when you're done.

2.44 Fill Handle

A fill handle is a function of Microsoft Excel that allows you to expand (and fill) a sequence of numbers, text, or even dates to a specified number of cells. The fill handle is a thin dark box in the lower right corner of the active cell in the spreadsheet, as seen in the picture. You can stretch the numbering chain down as many cells as you like if you insert the number "1" in the A1 cell and the number "2" in cell A2. You can do this by picking all cells and then using the left mouse button to click the fill handle (the little black box).

Drag the left cursor down the worksheet in column A while keeping the left mouse button pressed down. If you drag down to cell A60 and let go of the mouse button, cells A1 through A60 will now be numbered 1 to 60 in order without needing to type each number separately.

Entering" 5" into cell A1, then" 10" into cell A3, dragging a box across cells A1 through A4, and then dragging the fill handle down as far as you like is another way to use the fill handle. This sequence of events results in column A having 5, 10,15,20,25, and so on, with spaces between each cell.

2.45 Fill data automatically in worksheet cells

Fill cells with data that fits a trend or is dependent on data in other cells using the AutoFill function. Choose one or two cells to use as a starting point for filling additional cells. Form 1 and 2 in the first 2 cells for a sequence like 1, 2, 3, 4, 5... Type 2 and 4 for the sequence 2, 4, 6, 8, and so on. Form 2 just in the first cell for the sequence 2, 2, 2, 2... Drag the fill handle. If necessary, press the Auto Fill Option Button icon and choose the desired alternative.

2.46 Use of MS Excel spreadsheet

Spreadsheets are a crucial accounting and business instrument. They may be nuanced and used for a variety of purposes, but their main goal is to coordinate and categorize data in a logical manner. After you've inserted this information into the worksheet, you may use it to organize and expand the trade.

2.47 Some important shortcuts in MS excel

The print dialogue window can be opened by pressing Ctrl + P. A new workbook is generated by pressing Ctrl + N. The new workbook is saved by pressing Ctrl + S. Ctrl + C copies the contents of the currently selected object. Ctrl + V is a shortcut for pasting data from the clipboard. The feature insert dialogue window is opened by pressing SHIFT + F3. A new worksheet is generated by pressing SHIFT + F11.

Chapter 3: Data Filling and Sorting

When you've finished inserting data into your worksheet, you might want to filter it to make it simpler to access and scan. You may, for example, place a list of names in alphabetical or numerical order.

3.1 Data Sorting

In a column, you can sort data in an increasing or decreasing order.

To sort data in a list, do the following:

1. Press the column letter to choose the column you wish to sort.

2. Choose the Home tab from the dropdown menu.

3. In the Editing group, click the Sort and Filter tab.

4. Select whether you want the data to be ordered in ascending or descending order by clicking one of the buttons.

To rapidly organize the information:

- Choose a data set, such as A2:K6 (many columns and rows) or C2:C84 (a variety of rows and columns). The selection should include any titles you created to identify columns or rows.

- Choose one single cell inside the column in which you want to type.
- In Excel, choose the command that sorts A to Z, or the lowest number to the highest number, to perform an ascending type.
- In Excel, choose the command that filters Z to A, or the highest number to the lowest number to perform a descending type.

To sort the data according to a set of parameters:

- To sort a set, select a cell from anywhere inside it.
- Choose sort from the Filter & Sort group on the Data tab.
- A sorting dialogue box appears.
- From the Sort by Chart, choose the first column you want to focus on.
- From the Sort On the drop-down menu, choose Cell Icon, Values, Font Color, or Cell Color.
- From the Order chart, choose an order for the types: alphabetically, numerically ascending, or numerically descending or, in the case of percentages, lower to higher as well as higher to lower.

3.2 Complex Sorts

It's possible that you'll have to organize data over several columns. If your undergraduate class has been allocated team projects, for example, you might have a column for group names and a column for student names.

You should organize all the student names into project groups first, then alphabetize the student names within each project category. To filter by several columns, use the following steps:

1. Make a list of all the columns you would like to sort.

2. Choose the Home tab from the dropdown menu.

3. Choose Sort & Filter from the Editing party.

4. Choose Custom Sort from the dropdown menu. The Sort dialogue box will appear on the screen.

5. Pick the first column you would like to organize from the Column dropdown screen.

6. Pick A to Z from the Order dropdown menu to sort in ascending order or Z to A to sort in descending order from the Order dropdown menu.

7. For the remaining columns you want to sort, you'll need to create new tiers. By pressing the Add Level button and

selecting a level from the Then by dropdown screen, you can create a new level.

8. For each of the columns you wish to sort, enter the column's names and values.

9. Choose OK.

3.3 Autofill

You may use the Autofill function to easily fill cells with recurring or sequential details, such as repetitive text, dates, and numbers.

3.4 Autofill Dates

To Autofill a sequence of dates in a specific order, do the following:

1. In a cell, write the first date of the sequence.

2. Click the handle in the cell's bottom-right corner and pull it down to fill as many cells as you want.

3.5 Autofill Numbers

To Autofill a sequence of numbers in a specific order, do the following:

1. In a cell, write the first number in the sequence.

2. In the neighbouring cell, enter the 2nd number in the sequence.

3. Click and move the cursor over all cells to choose them.

4. To fill several cells, tap the handle in the lower right of the second cell and move it over as many cells as you like.

To automatically fill a row or column of cells with the same number or text:

1. Type the number/text into one of the cells.

2. Click and move the handle in the cell's bottom-right corner through as many cells as you would like to fill.

3.6 Using Autofill for alternating text and numbers

To fill several cells at once, use the autofill function. For example, type the seven days of the week into seven neighboring cells in a column or table, to create a repetitive list of the days of the week. Select the seven cells you want to fill, then press the handle in the lower right of the last cell and move it to as many cells as you want.

3.7 Functions of Autofill

Functions may be copied using Autofill. Columns A and B in the illustration below contain lists of numbers, while column C contains the total of columns A and B for each row. "=SUM(A2:B2)" will be the operation in cell C2. Follow these steps to copy this feature to the remaining cells in column C:

1. Find the cell that holds the feature you want to duplicate and double-click it. Cell C2 is picked in the illustration below.

	A	B	C	D	E
1	a	b	Total		
2	3	4	7		
3	6	6			
4	6	11			
5	10	3			
6	6	5			

C2 =SUM(A2:B2)

2. Click the handle in the cell's lower right and pull it down to fill as many cells as you want. For any of the rows chosen in the illustration below, the number of columns A and B will now be contained in column C.

	A	B	C	D	E
1	a	b	Total		
2	3	4	7		
3	6	6	12		
4	6	11	17		
5	10	3	13		
6	6	5	11		

C2 =SUM(A2:B2)

3.8 Filter the Data

- Pick the Data you want to filter.

- On the Data tab, choose Filter from the Sort and Filter category.

- Click the Filtering drop-down arrow in the column header to open a list of filter choices.

- To sort by values, uncheck the (Select All) check box in the chart. As a consequence, the checkmarks in any of the checkboxes are deleted. Then, to display the data, select the value you require and click OK.

3.9 How to delete Blank Rows

1. Select Find & Select from the Editing group on the Home tab.

2. Select Go To Special from the drop-down menu.

3. Click OK after selecting Blanks. The blank cells are now selected by Excel.

4. Select Delete from the Cells group on the Home tab.

5. Select Delete Sheet Rows from the drop-down menu.

3.10 Protect Workbook

In Excel, this example shows you how to secure the workbook structure.

1. Begin by opening a workbook.

2. Select Protect Workbook from the Protect category on the Review tab.

3. Click OK after checking Structure and entering a password.

Note: Excel 2013 and subsequent versions do not include the Windows option.

4. Click OK after reentering the password.

Users can no longer insert, remove, rename, move, copy, hide, or unhide worksheets once the workbook structure is protected.

To unlock the workbook, go to Protect Workbook and input the password. The password for the Excel file that may be downloaded is "easy."

3.11 Make the Workbook Read-only

This example demonstrates how to create a read-only workbook. Users may still save modifications to the worksheet by making a new copy. Protect a sheet for greater protection.

1. Begin by opening a workbook.

2. Select Save As from the File tab.

3. Select Browse from the menu.

4. Go to the Tools menu and choose General Options.

5. Type a password in the Password to Modify box and click OK.

Note: If you simply wish to suggest that people view the Excel file as read-only without safeguarding it, leave the password field blank and select Read-only advised.

6. Click OK after reentering the password.

Please keep in mind that this function does not encrypt your Excel file. Malicious individuals still would have the ability to change the file's contents and delete the password.

7. Give the file a name and save it.

Your workbook should now be read-only. The password for the Excel file that may be downloaded is "easy."

3.12 Make Meal Plan with Excel

This tutorial demonstrates how to make a meal plan in Excel. Here's what we're attempting to accomplish:

1. Make the following named ranges on the second sheet:

Breakfast A2:A10, Lunch B2:B10, and Dinner C2:C10

Note: You may add up to 7 additional morning meals without altering the range address in the future.

2. Select cell C4 on the first sheet.

3. Select Data Validation from the Data Tools category on the Data tab.

A dialogue box called 'Data Validation' opens.

4. Click List in the Allow box.

5. Type =Breakfast in the Source box.

6. Click OK to complete the process.

7. Repeat steps 2-6 for cells D4 and E4, using the Lunch and Dinner references in place of the Breakfast reference.

8. Drag the range C4:E4 down to row 10 and select it. The drop-down lists will be copied to the other days.

3.13 Calculate your BMI with Excel

The body mass index (BMI) is a weight-and-height-based measure of body fat that applies to men and women. Make an Excel BMI calculator to see whether you're at a healthy weight. Simply download the Excel file if you're in a rush.

A screenshot of the BMI calculator may be seen below.

Follow the instructions below to make the BMI calculator:

1. In cell C5, make a drop-down list.

2. To display the proper units, use an IF function in cells D7, D9, and D10.

3. From the drop-down menu, choose Metric. In cell D10, the IF function returns an empty string. When you choose Metric from the drop-down box, create conditional formatting rules that modify the format of cell C10 (steps 6, 7 and 8).

4. Formulate the BMI (Body Mass Index).

Explanation: The height in inches is calculated using C9*12+C10, while the height in meters is calculated using C9/100. BMI = 703*pounds/inches2 in standard units. BMI = kg/m2 as measured in metric values. The order in which computations are performed in Excel is set by default. If a portion of the formula is included in parentheses, it will be computed first. Remember that exponentiation () comes before multiplication (*) and division (/) in Excel.

5. Enter a 250-pound weight. Excel calculates the mass index (BMI) and changes the background color of the C13:E13 range automatically. Conditional formatting is the name for this functionality (steps 6, 7 and 8).

6. Select Conditional Formatting from the Styles category on the Home tab.

7. Select Manage Rules from the dropdown menu.

The Formatting Rules Manager for Conditional Formatting appears.

Change Current Selection to This Workbook from the drop-down list to see all conditional formatting rules in the workbook.

Note: To look more closely at each rule, pick it and click Edit Rule. The first four criteria relate to the BMI classifications. When you choose Metric from the drop-down list, the 5th rule alters the format of cell C10 (step 3).

Chapter 4: Excel formulas and functions

Excel's main features are its functions and formulas. Everything fascinating and helpful you'll ever have to work with in a worksheet is powered by them. This chapter covers the fundamental principles you'll need to remember in order to master Excel formulas. Here are a few examples.

4.1 What exactly is a formula?

In Excel, a formula is an equation that yields a given outcome. Consider the following example:

=2+2 // returns 4

=8/2 // returns 4

In Excel, all formulas must begin with the equals sign (=).

4.2 Cell references

Values are "hardcoded" in the cases above. This implies that until you update the formula again and adjust a value manually, the result will remain unchanged. This is often deemed unethical practice since it conceals facts and makes spreadsheet maintenance more difficult.

Use cell references instead so that values can be modified at any instant. Suppose D1 has the following formula:

=B1+ B2+ B3 // returns 12

Since cell references for B1, B2, and B3 are used, the values in these cells can be updated at any time, and D1 would always show a correct result.

Any formula yields a result.

Even if the outcome is a mistake, all formulas in Excel produce a result. To measure percent change, use the formula below. Since B4 is null, the formula returns a #DIV/0! Error in D4, but returns a right result in D2 and D3.

Errors may be dealt with in a variety of forms. In this scenario, you should either enter the missing value in B4 or use the IFERROR feature to "catch" the error and show a more polite note (or nothing at all).

4.3 Absolute and relative references

Relative references are what the cell references above are named. This indicates that the relationship is proportional to the cell in which it resides. The formula in E1 is as follows:

=B1+C1+D1 // formula in E1

As a result, as soon as the formula is written to cell F2, it tends to work correctly.

While relative references are incredibly helpful, there are occasions where a cell reference does not change. An absolute relation is a cell reference that does not alter when copied. Use the dollar sign ($) to render a comparison absolute:

=B1 // relative reference

=$B$1 // absolute reference

For instance, you would like to multiply each number in column D by 10, which is inserted in A1. You "lock" A1 by means of an absolute reference such that it doesn't alter when the formula is copied to F2 and F3:

Below are the final F1, F2, and F3 formulas:

=D1*$A$1 // formula in F1

=D2*$A$1 // formula in F2

=D3*$A$1 // formula in F3

When the formula is copied, the relation to D1 shifts, but the reference to A1 does not. You can now quickly adjust A1's value, and all 3 formulas can recalculate. The value in A1 has adjusted from 10 to 12.

This basic illustration also demonstrates that hardcoding values into a formula is not a good idea. By storing the value in A1 in a single location and referring to A1 with an absolute reference, the value may be updated at any time, and all related formulas will automatically update.

The F4 key can be used to switch between relative and absolute syntax.

4.4 Formulas may be copied and pasted

Cell references are useful since they immediately refresh when a formula is copied to a different location. This eliminates the need to repeatedly enter the same simple formula. Control + C has been used to copy the formula in E1 to the clipboard:

Control + V was used to paste the formula into cell E2. It's worth noting that the cell references have been adjusted:

E3 was pasted with the same formula. The following cell phone numbers have been updated:

4.5 What is the best way to enter a formula?

To insert a formula, follow these steps:

1. Choose a cell.

2. Type the equals symbol (=).

3. Click enter after typing the formula.

You may point and click rather than typing cell references. It's worth noting that the references are color-coded.

In Excel, all formulas must start with an equals sign (=). If there is no equals symbol, there is no formula.

4.6 How should you alter a formula?

You have three choices for editing a formula:

1. Choose the cell and change the formula in the formula bar.

2. Update the cell directly by double-clicking it.

3. Select the cell, click F2, and edit it right away.

When you're done, click Enter to validate your adjustments, regardless of which choice you choose. Click the Escape key to cancel the operation and leave the formula unchanged.

4.7 Connecting Worksheets

You may use data from two separate worksheets to construct a formula. This may be achieved either inside a single workbook or through several workbooks. When joining cells from worksheets inside the same workbook, the main formula is inscribed as "sheetsname!cellsaddress". When connecting cells from multiple workbooks, the main formula is written as "[workbookdname.xlsx]sheetsname!cellsaddress". The formula "=B1+Sheet2!A2" can be used to incorporate the values of cell B1 in Worksheet 2 and cell A2 in Worksheet 3. If Worksheet 2 was in Book2.xlsx and Worksheet 3 was in Book3.xlsx, the exact same cells might be inserted with the formula "=[Book2.xlsx]Sheet2!$A$2+A3." In this instance, the formula will be entered on Sheet 3 of Book3.xlsx.

4.8 What is a function?

When working in Excel, the terms "formula" and "function" are often used interchangeably. They are similar, but they are not identical. A formula is described as an expression that starts with the equals sign (=).

In contrast, a function is a formula with a unique name and meaning. In most instances, roles are named after the purpose for which they were created. Excel has hundreds of different functions. For instance, you're probably familiar with the SUM feature, which provides the sum of two or more references:

=SUM(1,2,4) // returns 7

=SUM(B1:B3) // returns B1+B2+B3

As you would assume, the AVERAGE function determines the average of the specified references:

=AVERAGE(3,12,3) // returns 6

The MIN and MAX functions, respectively, return the minimum and maximum values:

=MIN(2,3,4) // returns 2

=MAX(2,3,4) // returns 4

4.9 Arguments of functions

To return an output, most functions need inputs. These are referred to as "arguments." The arguments to a function exist within parentheses after the function term, divided by commas. Open and closed parentheses are used for all functions (). The pattern looks like the following:

=FUNCTIONNAME(argument1,argument2,argument3)

The COUNTIF function, for example, counts cells that follow a set of requirements and takes two statements, range and criteria:

=COUNTIF(range,criteria) // two arguments

The range on the screen is A1:A6, and the criterion is "green." In C1, the formula is:

=COUNTIF(A1:A6,"green") // returns 2

All the arguments are not needed. Optional arguments are displayed in square brackets. The YEARFRAC function, for example, returns the fractional no. of years between two dates and takes three arguments:

=YEARFRAC(start_date,end_date,[basis])

The start and end dates are necessary arguments, while the basis is optional for an explanation of how to use YEARFRAC to measure current age-dependent on birthdate.

4.10 How to enter a function?

Simply start typing if you already know the function's name. The steps are as follows:

Type the equals symbol (=) and then begin typing. When you type, Excel will generate a list of matching functions:

Use the arrow keys to pick the function you want from the options (or just continue typing).

To approve a function, press the Tab key. The function will be completed by Excel:

Fill in the blanks with the requisite arguments:

To validate the calculation, press Enter.

4.11 Nesting (Combining Functions)

Many Excel formulas have several features, which can be "nested" within each other. For instance, suppose you have a C1 birthdate and want to measure the current age in C2:

YEARFRAC is a function that calculates years that have a start and finish date:

B1 can be used for the start date, and the TODAY feature can be used for the end date:

You can get your current age depending on today's date when you click Enter to confirm:

=YEARFRAC(B1,TODAY())

You'll see that you're feeding an end date to the YEARFRAC feature using the TODAY function. To put it another way, the TODAY function may be used to include the end date statement for the YEARFRAC function. You may take the formula another step forward by chopping off the decimal value with the INT function:
=INT(YEARFRAC(B1,TODAY()))

The INT function receives 20.4 from the YEARFRAC formula, and the INT function returns a final value of 20.

Observations

1. In the pictures above, the latest date is February 22, 2019.

2. The best example of nesting functions is nested IF functions.

3. The TODAY feature is a unique Excel function since it doesn't need any arguments.

4.12 Math Operators

The standard math operators currently offered in Excel are listed in the table below:

Operation	Symbol	Example
Subtraction	-	=9-3=6
Addition	+	=3+3=6
Division	/	=12/4=3
Multiplication	x	=4x2=8
Parentheses	()	=(2+7)/3=3
Exponentiation	^	=4^2=16

4.13 Logical operators

Comparative analysis such as "greater than," "less than," and so on are supported by logical operators. The table below lists the logical operators easily accessible in Excel:

Meaning	Operator	Example
Equal to	=	=A1=10
Not equal to	<>	=A1<>10
Greater than	>	=A1>100
Less than	<	=A1<100
Greater than or equal to	>=	=A1>=75
Less than or equal to	<=	=A1<=0

4.14 Order of operations

The performance of some formulas and functions may be directly fed into another function or formula as a key takeaway. The sequence of events is as follows:

Excel assumes an "order of operations" pattern when solving a formula. Any sentences in parentheses must first be checked. Excel can then determine any exponents that might exist. Excel can execute multiplication and division after exponents, followed by addition and subtraction. Concatenation can occur after regular math operations if the formula requires it. Finally, if logical operators are present, Excel may test them.

4.15 To convert formulas to values

Often you get sick of formulas and want to replace them with ideals. In Excel, the simplest method is to copy the formula and then paste it using Paste Special > Values. This replaces the values returned by the formulas. You will paste values using a keyboard shortcut or the Paste menu on the Home tab of the Ribbon.

4.16 Top 10 Basic Excel Functions

Basic Functions in Microsoft Excel are Excel's most significant functions. It aids you in doing both simple and complicated calculations. Here is a list of 10 basic Excel functions that you can master:

1. Sum

This function returns the total of all the digits in a cell. You may either refer to the values in the cells or simply enter them into the function.

2. Count

This is a function that returns the number of numeric values in a cell. You may either refer to the values in the cells or simply enter them into the function.

3. Average

This function calculates the average of numeric values in a cell. You may either refer to the values in the cells or simply enter them into the function.

4. Time

This function generates a correct time serial number in Excel's time format. Hours, minutes, and seconds must be defined.

5. Date

This returns a valid date serial number in the format of Excel. You must state the day, month, and year.

6. Left

Beginning from the left, this feature removes unique characters from a cell/string (start). You must define the text to be extracted, as well as the number of characters to be extracted.

7. Right

Beginning from the right, this feature removes basic characters from a cell/string (last). You must define the text to be extracted, as well as the number of characters to be extracted.

8. VLookup

This function searches a column for a value and may return the value or a value from the adjacent columns of the same row number. If a condition is TRUE, this function returns a number, and if the condition is FALSE, it returns another value.

9. Now

This displays the latest time and date in the cell where you type it in using your system's settings.

10. Creating a basic formula in Microsoft Excel

To incorporate, delete, multiply, or divide values in your worksheet, you should use a simple formula. Simple formulas often begin with an equal sign (=), accompanied by numeric constants and measurement operators like plus (+), an asterisk (*), minus (-), and forward-slash (/).

4.17 Excel Formulas

Let's look at a basic formula as an example.

- Click the cell where you'd like to write the formula on the worksheet.
- Type the equal sign (=) accompanied by the operators and constants you choose to use in the equation (upto 8192 characters). Type =2+2 in our case.
- Press Enter (on a PC) or Return (on a Mac).

Let's look at another example of a basic formula. In a different cell, type =5+2*3 and click Enter or Return. Excel adds the first number to the calculation of multiplying the last two figures.

4.18 Use of AutoSum

To easily sum a column, line, or set of numbers, use AutoSum. Select a cell in front of the numbers you would like to add, go to the Home page, select AutoSum, and then press Enter in Windows or Return in Mac. Excel immediately enters a formula (using the SUM feature) to add the numbers when you press AutoSum. Choose one or even more cells to use as a starting point for filling in additional cells.

Type 1 and 2 in the first 2 cells for a sequence like 1, 2, 3, 4, 5... Type 2 and 4 for the sequence 2, 4, 6, 8, and so on. Form 2 just in the first cell for the sequence 2,2,2, 2... Complete the handle by dragging it. If necessary, press the Auto Fill Options Button icon and choose the desired alternative.

4.19 Useful formulas for everyday activities

While the names of the five formulas below are a little confusing, their role is to enter data on a regular basis and save time.

Note: Certain formulas enable you to enter the text or values you want to be measured in a single cell or set. You may either manually input the cell/range address, or use the cursor to point to it as Excel shows the multiple cell/range dialogue boxes. When you point, you first press the field box, then the corresponding cell in the worksheet. For formulas that quantify a range of cells, repeat the procedure (e.g., starting date, ending date, etc.).

1. =DAYS =

This is a useful method for calculating the no. of days between 2 dates (so you don't have to worry about the number of days in each month of the range).

Example: End Date Septmber 12, 2015 minus Start Date February 28, 2015 = 192 days.

Formula: =DAYS(A30,A29)

2. NETWORK DAYS =

This method measures the number of workdays (i.e., five days per week) in a given amount of time. It also has a feature that allows you to exclude holidays from the number, although this must be done as a range of dates.

Example: Start Date March 31, 2021 minus End Date October 12, 2021 = 140 days.

=NETWORKDAYS is a formula for calculating the number of days in a network (A33,A34).

3. =Trim

If you're always importing or pasting text into Excel (such as from a word processing software, website, database, or other text-based programs), TRIM is a huge help. Frequently, the imported text contains extra spaces scattered around the list. TRIM eliminates the excess spaces in a matter of seconds. Simply insert the formula once and copy it to the end of the list.

=TRIM plus the cell address enclosed in parenthesis, for example.

Formula: =TRIM(A39)

4. Concatenate

If you upload a large amount of data into Excel, this is another must-have. This formula combines the contents of 2 or more fields/cells into a single field/cell. Consider the following scenario: Dates, hours, contact numbers, and other multiple data documents are often entered in different fields in databases, which is inconvenient. Simply surround this data with quotation marks to add gaps between terms, or punctuation between areas.

=CONCATENATE plus (month," space," day," comma space," year), where the month, day, and year are cell addresses, and the information within the quotation marks is a space and a comma.

Formula: For dates enter: =CONCATENATE(E38," ",F38,", ",G38)

Formula: For phone numbers enter: =CONCATENATE(E39,"-",F39,"-",G39)

5. =Datevalue

Datevalue transforms the above-mentioned formula into an Excel date, which you'll use if you're going to use it for calculations. This one is simple: From the formula collection, choose DATEVALUE. In the dialogue box, click the Date Text sector, then click the respective cell on the spreadsheet, click OK, and copy down. Since the data are Excel serial numbers, go to format>Format Cells>Number>Date and pick a format from the drop-down menu.

Formula: =DATEVALUE(H32)

6. =FORMULATEXT

This feature is used to show the "text" of a formula in a cell. In cell E2, for example, the exact formula is =SUM(C2*D2), but you only see the result, which is $164.25. When editing macros or finding a circular comparison, it's often useful, if not important, to see the actual feature. So type =FORMULATEXT(E2) into a cell off to the edge of your spreadsheet matrix (like cell F2), and Excel will present the E2 formula.

7. =AVERAGE

Averages are used to find the median as well as the midpoint of a series of figures, such as average grades for a group of pupils, the average temperature for an area, and/or average height of seventh graders. To get an average before functions, you can add a column of numbers, say 10 numbers, and then divide by that sum (10). This is handled by the AVERAGE function. As a result, typing =AVERAGE(E1:E6) brings the six numbers together, then divides them by six.

8. =Count & =CountA

These straightforward functions count the cumulative amount of digits or characters in a data column. COUNTA counts all, including alpha and numeric characters, punctuation, letters, and even spaces, while COUNT only counts numbers and formulas.

Why would you choose to use the COUNT function? Assume that friends have paid fees to join various parties. The fees for all clubs are added to column G in the database, so each member knows how much he or she owes each month. To total, the number of people in each club, use the COUNT feature. For, e.g., =COUNT(B12:B21) informs that the Garden Club has six members.

9. =COUNTBLANK

The COUNTBLANK feature does just as it says; it counts how many blank cells there are in a column or set. There are four blank cells in column C of our spreadsheet example (and six cells with numbers). It's worth noting that everything in a cell, even space, counts as a non-blank cell. In other terms, putting a gap in cell C13 reduces the number of blank cells from four to three.

10. COUNTIF AND COMBINED FUNCTIONS

To count the number of cells in a set that satisfies a given requirement, this formula incorporates the COUNT and IF functions.

For example, suppose you choose to list the number of participants in a Music Club (column C), but only those who pay the $18.00 monthly membership fee. You count the cells first, then set the condition, as in =COUNTIF(C13:C22, "18"). Note: If you don't place the criteria within double quotes, you'll get an error message.

You may also merge different roles to get the results you like, so you don't have to waste valuable spreadsheet space by using multiple cells or columns. Consider a situation where you need to identify how many cells with numbers (or text) plus blanks are in a column or cell.

Enter the following formula for the numbers and the blanks:

=COUNT(C13:C22) + COUNTBLANK(C13:C22)

Enter the following equations for all characters (numeric and alpha) plus the blanks: =COUNTA(C13:C22) + COUNTBLANK(C13:C22)

11.=TRANSPOSE

If you want to move the spreadsheet's field rows to columns or vice versa, this is a really useful function. Why would anyone need to do this? When creating spreadsheets, if you aren't really sure, the details should be the fields, which should be the information, and the condition can shift, necessitating a redesign. The Transpose feature comes in handy here.

First, pick a set of blank cells that is the same size as the initial range underneath (or on another sheet). It's worth noting that the initial number of columns/fields was possibly six, whereas the number of rows/records was possibly seven. You'll have seven columns and six rows when you transpose the results, so make sure your blank cells represent that. The original range of highlighted blank cells could be A32:E38, but the current range of highlighted blank cells should be A40:E45.

Form =TRANSPOSE(A32:E39) in the highlighted segment to use the initial range coordinates. Once you've reached the feature and range, click Ctrl+Shift-Enter, and the range will adjust right in front of your eyes.

12.=MAX & =MIN

These two are straightforward, but they're really helpful. If you need to find the maximum or minimum number of things in a column or row, move your cursor beyond the matrix and use the following functions: =MAX(D33:D37) or =MIN(E33:E37). The largest or lowest number in the column list is returned by Excel.

There are three further formula suggestions.

Tip 1: To translate formulas to text or numbers, you don't need another formula. Simply copy the formula set and paste it as Special>Values. What's the point of converting calculations to numbers? Data can't be moved or manipulated before it's transformed. Some cells can seem to be phone numbers, but they're formulas that can't be manipulated as numbers or email.

Tip 2: If you paste a date into Copy and Paste > Special > Values, the output would be code, which cannot be translated to a real date. To behave as actual dates, the DATEVALUE formula is needed.

Tip 3: Formulas are often shown in uppercase, but Excel transforms them to lowercase if you type them in lowercase. It's also worth noting that formulations are devoid of spaces. If the formula fails, look for and delete any spaces.

Chapter 5: Charts and Graphs

Using a number of chart forms, charts enable you to display data inserted into a spreadsheet in a graphic format. You should first enter data into a spreadsheet before you create a chart or graph.

5.1 How to create a chart?

To make a graph, follow these steps:

1. Enter the required information into a spreadsheet.

2. Choose the cells, including the headings that you wish to use in the chart.

3. Press the Insert button. Excel offers a variety of chart types in the Charts category, including column, pie, bar, line, area, scatter, and other charts.

4. Once you've selected a chart type, a menu will appear, displaying additional chart types for that form.

5. Choose the chart type you'd like to use. The chart will appear in your spreadsheet.

5.2 Chart Resizing

To resize your graph, follow these steps:

1. Select the chart by clicking on it. Around the chart box, an eight-handle boundary should emerge.

2. Drag the chart to its current height by clicking one of the handles.

5.3 Moving a Chart

To switch the chart to a different position on your spreadsheet, follow these steps:

1. Select the chart by clicking on it.

2. Move the mouse across the chart box's boundary until the cursor changes to a ⊕.

3. Drag the chart to its new position by clicking and dragging it.

5.4 Moving chart elements

You may also change the order of the chart's features, such as the labels, title, and graphics. To transfer elements inside a chart, do the following:

1. Choose the element you would like to transfer by clicking it. It will be surrounded by a border.

2. Continue to move the mouse across the boundary until the pointer changes to a ⊕.

3. Drag and drop the element into its new place.

5.5 Formatting a Chart

The Chart Tools bar will be displayed around the Ribbon once you've built a chart or picked a chart. The Design, Layout, and Format tabs on the Chart Tools bar are helpful for editing and customizing your chart. The Layout tab helps you adjust a chart's axes and gridlines, align the legend and labels, and display the chart's context. You can adjust the layout of your chart using the Design tab. You may adjust the type of your chart components, such as the text types and shape, using the Format tab. A brief list of more basic features that can be accessed from the Layout, Design, and Format tabs is provided below.

Format Selection – To format an item on the chart, press the object on the chart or choose the object from the Format tab's Chart Elements dropdown menu. A window with the object's properties will open, allowing you to make formatting adjustments.

Chart Type – On the Design tab, press the Alter Chart Type button to modify the chart form.

Legend – The Map Legend icon, found on the Layout page, lets you choose where the legend appears on the chart and whether or not it is visible.

Show Data by Column or Row – On the Design tab, press the Switch Row/Column button to display the data by column or row.

5.6 Copying a Chart to Microsoft Word

Take these measures to copy a completed chart into a Microsoft Word document:

1. Press the chart to choose it.

2. Select Copy.

3. Open the Microsoft Word document into which you'd like to insert the graph.

4. Choose Paste.

5.7 Incorporate a Graphic into a Chart

You may create a graphic picture of the Chart's background using the Illustrations tab on the Insert side. It can be done with a dataset dot, but it's normally easier to do it with a larger part of the Chart, such as the plot field. Data identifiers, like the rows/columns in a rows/columns table, may also provide graphics. You may extend the graphic over the whole row or stack the picture up to the height of the row/column.

5.8 Change the Axis Scale

There are four values on the y-axis scale: minimum, major unit, minor unit, and maximum. The minimum and maximum values are the smallest and largest tick points that appear on the axes. The key instrument is the increasing value in-between the scale's dashed line.

The small tick marks are the second set of tick marks on the Chart that may or may not be highlighted; whether they are is determined by the small unit sense. Major tick marks occur in front of an axis value, whereas tiny tick marks do not show in front of an axis value if they are available. The Layout Axis (Horizontal) dialogue box is seen in this graphic. It is positioned on the right hand side of the excel spreadsheet.

Chapter 6: XML to Excel Conversion

The XML file format is widely used on the internet, and you will need to deal with the data contained in an XML file at some point.

It is no longer necessary to use the XML file explicitly since it was not designed to be interpreted by humans but by machines. However, in this scenario, knowing how to convert an XML file to Excel would enable you to interact with and evaluate the data more easily.

6.1 What is an XML file?

XML is an acronym for "Extensible Markup Language." An XML file should store data in a format that applications and systems can understand.

However, humans find it difficult to read, so it will need to be converted into a more user-friendly style.

If the XML file includes a large amount of text data, you can read it using a text editor; if it involves numerical data, you can import it into Excel and deal with the data there.

XML is a commonly used file format for storing and transmitting data over the internet. The XML file format is used for several common file formats, including

Microsoft Office Open XML, OpenDocument, LibreOffice, XHTML, and SVG.

The sitemaps of the majority of prominent websites on the internet are in XML format. This is a file that includes information on any of a website's relevant sites and categories. Forbes also included an overview of a sitemap.

Let's look at how to use Power Query to transform an XML file to Excel.

6.2 Excel XML File Import

You can quickly translate an XML file into data in an Excel file if you already have one (either downloaded or linked to on the web).

Power Query (now named 'Get and Transform') is to thank for this.

Import an XML file that has been saved on your computer.

When you have the XML file opened on your device, take the steps below to import the data from the XML file into Excel:

1. Open the Excel tab where you want the data from the XML file to be extracted to.

2. Go to the Data page.

3. Select the 'Get Data' alternative from the 'Get & Transform' data group.

4. Select 'From file' from the drop-down menu.

5. Select 'From XML' from the drop-down menu.

6. Locate and pick the XML file you wish to import in the input data dialogue box that appears.

7. Import should be selected. This will open the Navigator dialogue box and import the XML file into PowerQuery.

8. Choose the data you would like to import from the XML format. In this scenario, you can go to the left pane and press on 'sitemap'.

9. If you need to convert the data before loading it into Excel, click the Transform Data icon. (Adjust the column labels or delete any columns, for example.)

10. Select Load.

In the Excel file, the above steps will create a fresh worksheet and load all the data from the XML file into it.

The benefit of using Power Query to extract data from an XML file into Excel is that you don't have to repeat the process if the XML file changes and new records are added.

You can refresh the query by right-clicking on any cell in the table.

6.3 Using the web URL, import an XML file into Excel

You don't really need to download the file if you have a domain URL that includes the XML file. You can use Power Query to connect to that URL and then export the XML data to Excel.

The steps for connecting PowerQuery to a web URL that includes XML data and importing that data into Excel are as follows:

1. Open the Excel file that contains the details you intend to import.

2. Go to the Data page.

3. Select the 'Get Data' option from the Get & Transform group.

4. Select 'Other Sources' from the drop-down menu.

5. Select 'From Web' from the drop-down menu.

6. Copy/paste the XML data URL into the 'From Web' dialogue box.

7. When you click OK, the Navigator dialogue box will appear, allowing you to choose which XML data to import.

8. Select 'sitemap,' which is the XML data needed in Excel.

9. If you would like to convert the data before loading it into Excel, click the Transform Data icon. (Adjust the column titles or delete any columns, for example.)

10. Select Load.

In the Excel file, the above steps will create a fresh worksheet and load all the data from the XML file into it.

If the data in this URL changes, just refresh the link to get the updated data in Excel.

So those are the two basic methods for converting an XML file to Excel.

Chapter 7: Troubleshooting MS Excel 2021

Most individuals are either low on time and have a deadline to reach while dealing with Excel spreadsheets, making it a disaster if Microsoft Excel refuses to launch at any stage.

Unfortunately, when Excel declines to open one of the essential Excel files or refuses to open the Excel program at all, this behavior is very normal. So, if you're experiencing the dreaded 'Microsoft Excel won't open' issue, this chapter is for you.

Here is a guide that will go through the explanations of why Excel won't open and what you should do about it.

7.1 Possible Reasons for not opening of MS Excel

There are aspects that may go wrong in Excel as it is a platform that must function together with other software and operating systems. Of course, it's also possible that the Excel program is the source of the issue.

The following are several potential causes for Microsoft Excel not opening on your computer:

1. You are unable to open Excel files due to a malfunctioning add-in. If this is the case, you would most definitely be able to open Excel programs but not individual Excel files or a new one.

2. There's a chance the Excel program is corrupt, and you'll need to patch it before you can access Excel files again.

3. The Excel program is unable to interact with other programs or the operating system. This is an easy fix; simply allow the configuration, and your files can begin to function again (covered later in this chapter).

4. The file association is disabled, which ensures it doesn't know what program to use to access an Excel file when you want to open it. You can easily correct this by merely resetting the file associations. This is a common problem with people who have updated their Excel or operating system.

5. The file you're trying to access is corrupted. This also occurs when you share a file with someone else or copy a file to an external drive or to a network drive and then move it to your device. There's not anything you can do about this situation except make sure you back up your data in the future.

7.2 How to Open Excel Files That Won't Open

Let's have a peek at some of the approaches for resolving the problem of Excel files not opening. These corrections are listed in the order in which they are most likely to perform.

7.3 Uncheck the box that says "Ignore DDE".

The most popular and simplest solution is to ensure that the proper setting for Dynamic Data Exchange is allowed (DDE).

DDE is the method by which Excel communicates with other programs.

The DDE setting is disabled by default, but if it is allowed by mistake, it can prevent your Excel files from opening on your device.

You'll be able to access the Excel program from the start menu, but you won't be able to open specific Excel files if this occurs.

The measures to resolve the DDE problem are as follows:

1. From the Start menu, choose the Excel file.
2. Go to the File Tab.
3. Choose Options.

4. In the Excel Options dialogue box that appears on the left pane, press the 'Advanced' button.

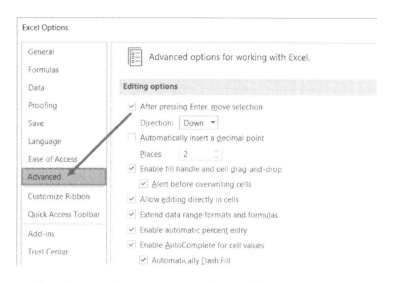

5. Go to the General portion and scroll down.

6. Disable the option to ignore other programs that use Dynamic Data Exchange (DDE).

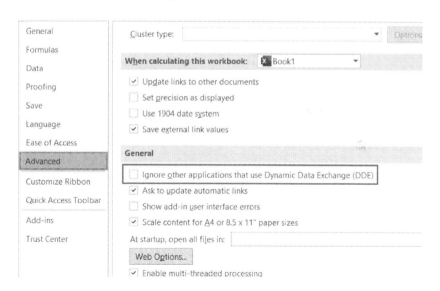

7. Exit the Excel Options window.

If this configuration was previously allowed and you removed it using the measures above, this was most definitely the issue, which should now be resolved.

Continue reading if this approach doesn't fix your issue.

7.4 How to turn off Ads-in

Many people use third-party Excel add-ins to extend the capabilities and allow them to use several features that aren't available by default in Excel.

One of the add-ins is 'ThinkCell,' which helps to make beautiful graphs and charts that are not achicvable with Excel alone. These add-ins can also be the cause of you being unable to access your Excel files. Disabling the add-in is the simple solution.

The following are the measures to uninstall an add-on in Excel:

1. From the Start menu, choose the Excel file.

2. Go to the File Tab.

3. Select Options.

4. Hit the Add-ins icon in the left pane of the Excel Options dialogue window.

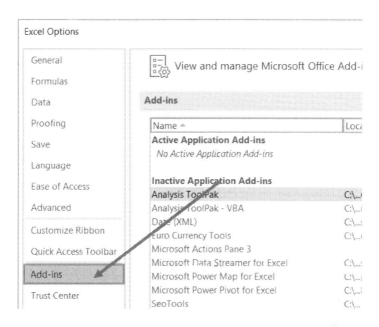

5. Click the Manage menu at the base of the dialogue box.

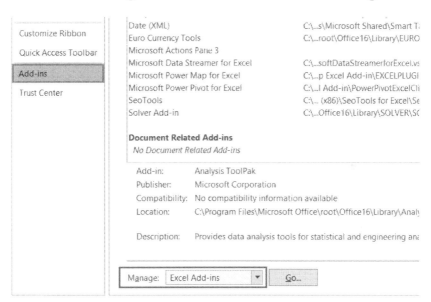

6. Select COM Add-ins from the drop-down menu.

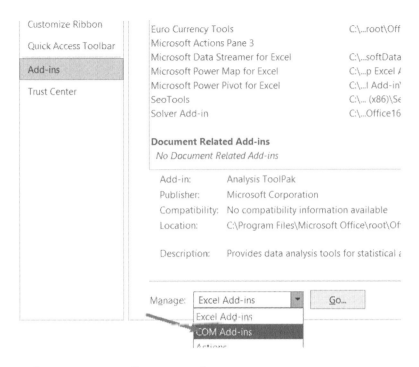

7. Go by pressing the Enter key.

8. Disable all add-ins in the COM Add-ins dialogue box that appears.

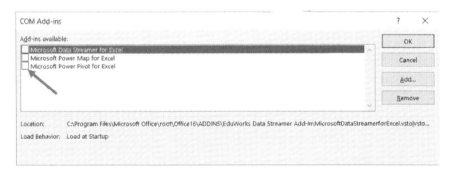

9. Click the OK button.

Now try to access an Excel file that wouldn't open previously. If this was the issue then the file should open normally.

Often, it's a one-time thing, and the add-in can continue to function normally if you activate it again. If you allow the add-in and the issue persists, it is likely that the add-in is corrupt and has to be permanently removed.

7.5 Microsoft Office can be repaired

Another explanation Excel files aren't opening is because the Microsoft Office program is corrupt and needs to be restored or reinstalled. But, as reinstalling is a bit more effort, let's start with the repair alternative.

To restore the Microsoft Office program on your device, follow the measures below:

1. Press the R key when holding down the Windows key. The 'Run' dialogue box will appear.

2. Type the command 'appwiz.cpl' into the run box. This will bring up the dialogue box for programs and functions.

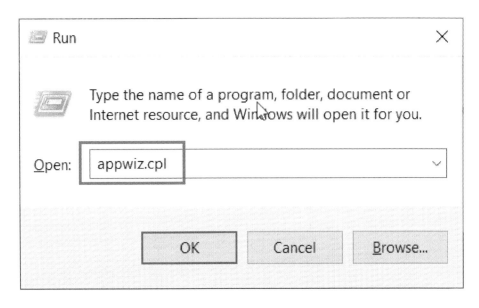

3. Choose Microsoft Office from the drop-down menu.

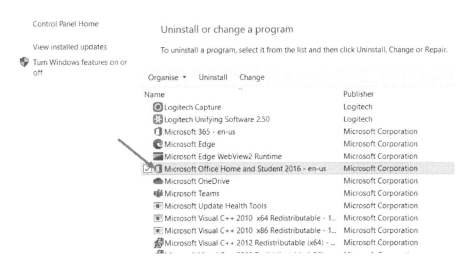

4. Change the Microsoft Office option by right-clicking on it. (If you see the button to repair right here, choose it.)

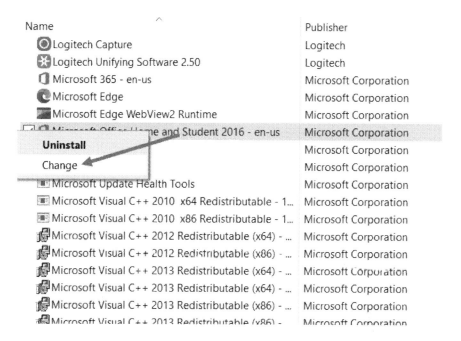

5. In the resulting dialogue box, choose the Quick Repair method.

6. Choose Repair from the drop-down menu.

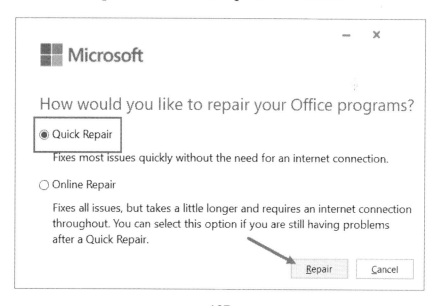

Follow the on-screen instructions to repair your Microsoft Office program in a matter of minutes.

If the problem was caused by a compromised Microsoft Office program, following the measures above will resolve it.

Let's look at some more fixes if you're still having trouble opening Excel data.

7.6 Excel File Associations Can Be Reset

When you launch an Excel file, the file association ensures that the Excel application is used to open it. And, occasionally, these file associations go wrong, so when you press on an Excel file, it doesn't recognize that it needs to be opened with the Excel application.

Resetting file associations is the solution.

The steps to accomplish this, are as follows:

1. To begin, open the Control Panel.

2. Go to Programs and select it.

Adjust your computer's settings   View by: Categ

 System and Security
Review your computer's status
Save backup copies of your files with File History
Back up and Restore (Windows 7)

 Network and Internet
View network status and tasks

 Hardware and Sound
View devices and printers
Add a device
Adjust commonly used mobility settings

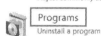 **Programs**
Uninstall a program

 User Accounts
Change account type

 Appearance and Personalisation

 Clock and Region
Change date, time or number formats

 Ease of Access
Let Windows suggest settings
Optimise visual display

3. Select Default Programs from the drop-down menu.

Choose the programs that Windows uses by default

 Set your default programs
Make a program the default for all file types and protocols that it can open.

 Associate a file type or protocol with a program
Make a file type or protocol always open in a specific program.

 Change AutoPlay settings
Play CDs or other media automatically

 Set program access and computer defaults
Control access to certain programs and set defaults for this computer.

4. Select 'Set your default programs' from the drop-down menu.

 Programs and Features
Uninstall a program | Turn Windows features on or off | View installed updates
Run programs made for previous versions of Windows | How to install a program

Default Programs
Change default settings for media or devices

5. Scroll to the 'Reset to the Microsoft recommended defaults' section of the Default apps window that appears and click the Reset button.

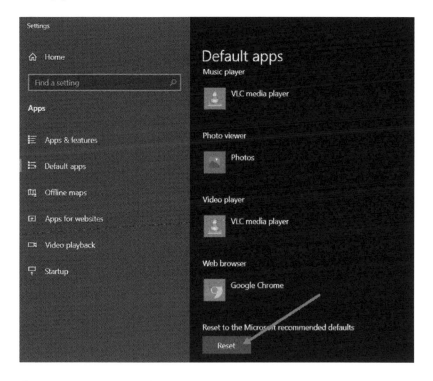

6. If a mismatched file association was preventing your Excel files from opening, this will solve the problem.

Because we've reset the default for all the applications on your device, any manual changes you've made, such as specifying a particular file extension to be launched with a particular application, will be reset to the default as well.

If you don't want to reset the default for all applications but only for Excel files, Click the 'choose default applications by file types' option.

Find the Excel file extensions (.xls,.csv,.xlsx,.xlsb,. etc.) and make XLS the default software for those in the screen that appears.

7.7 Turning off Hardware Graphic Acceleration

It improves the performance of your device, particularly with Microsoft Products like MS Word or MS Excel.

However, this will sometimes result in your Excel files not working, or cause your device or files to crash.

So, if everything else fails, this strategy is worth a shot.

The problem can be resolved by removing hardware graphic amplification, which is allowed by design.

Here are the steps to follow:

1. Launch the Excel programs.

2. Choose the File page.

3. Choose Options.

4. In the Excel Options dialogue box that appears, in the left pane, press the Advanced button.

5. Go to the 'Display' settings and scroll down.

6. Choose – 'Display hardware graphic acceleration' from the drop-down menu.

7. Choose OK.

Your Excel files should now open if hardware graphic acceleration was the issue.

There's just so much you can do in terms of troubleshooting.

If nothing else seems to be working, you can contact Microsoft support to see if they can assist you.

More often than not, these problems can be traced back to a Microsoft update that was published recently, which unwittingly triggered the issue.

Another option is to post your question on one of the several active Microsoft forums, where the wonderful people of the Internet can assist you.

Chapter 8: Applications of MS Excel 2021

Many features, algorithms, and shortcuts are included in the Excel software package that can be used to improve its functionality.

The following are some of Excel's uses:

- Entry of data
- Management of data
- Financial evaluation
- Customer relationship management (CRM)
- Graphing and charting
- Computer programming
- Managing the time
- Regulation of tasks
- Financial simulations
- Accounting

Almost everything that needs organization!

8.1 Financial and accounting uses

Excel is widely used in the banking and accounting fields. In reality, many businesses depend solely on Excel spreadsheets for their budgeting, planning, and accounting needs.

Although Excel is a "data" processing method, the most popular data that is handled is financial data. Excel is the ultimate financial software, according to CFI. Although there are several parts of financial software that are designed to execute complex functions, Excel's robustness and openness are its best features. Excel templates can be as efficient as the analyst wants.

8.2 The Most Valuable Business Advantages of Microsoft Excel

All companies must expand and progress in order to remain successful in today's environment. One strategy is to remain ahead of the competition by promoting profitability and implementing growth strategies, thus ensuring employees stay on top of new technologies and perform as efficiently as possible.

Employees who are talented deserve to be put to the test and strive tirelessly to remain ahead of the game. Employers can boost morale and reduce attrition by providing employees with the preparation and training they need to achieve their goals. They will also reduce the chance of losing highly qualified workers to competitors by providing them with the continuing preparation they require to be as productive as they want. Excel for a company is a common curriculum in education training.

8.3 What is the aim of Excel?

Excel helps consumers calculate, organize, and view objective statistics, giving administrators and senior personnel the knowledge they need to make rational choices that would have an effect on the organization. Employees who are proficient in advanced Excel functions will be able to describe their data to upper management more efficiently. It's also a requisite ability for employees who wish to advance in their careers.

Advanced Excel skills will help both employees and employers. Let's look at the advantages of using Excel as part of a company's daily employee training.

8.4 Excel's Employee Benefits

Employees may benefit from advanced Excel preparation in a number of areas, including growing their value and discovering different resources to improve their job results.

8.5 Making Improvements to The Skill Set

You must strive to practice and develop your abilities in order to succeed in your career. Advanced Excel preparation encompasses a wide range of valuable skills that can be used and enjoyed in practically every work position. After some practice, you will be able to:

- Analyse, manipulate, and evaluate results.
- Create equations that can provide you with more data on important business functions such workflow, project efficiency, financial projections and budgets, and maybe inventory levels and usage.
- Provide simple data collection that top management can use to determine existing tasks or situations in the company.
- Create spreadsheets to better coordinate details to see what's been entered more clearly.
- Interpret and comprehend details and spreadsheets from other organizations, vendors, and customers.
- Have the ability to see details at a deeper level which helps you find answers and alternatives to market issues.
- Manage complex financial and product documents by planning, balancing, and maintaining them.

- Set up control programs for separate agencies and operations and also multiple workflow procedures.

Advanced Microsoft Excel training can often provide managers with higher-skilled jobs, as well as ways to assist staff in working more effectively in their new roles and preparing them for promotion to higher-level positions.

8.6 Improving The Data Organization

Spreadsheets are widely used for data collection and organization. In the simplest form, Excel is a spreadsheet program. It assists you in carefully organizing data while still encouraging you to enter the data in whatever manner you want. Data at its most basic state can be perplexing and impossible to comprehend. You'll be able to better arrange the data, conduct calculations as needed, and sort the data so that it can be properly interpreted and converted to graphs and charts for easier viewing using Excel's advanced features.

8.7 Productivity and Efficiency Enhancement

Excel is a vital method for increasing productivity and allowing employees to be more efficient while dealing with vast amounts of data and measurements. You will be able to utilize Excel's more sophisticated features, which could help you complete assignments and interpret data more efficiently once you have a better understanding of the program. This will also allow you to keep team members up to date with data, which will accelerate the workflow phase.

Even better, studying advanced Excel can help you make your calculations more effective. Calculations that must be replicated take time, particularly if you must double-check your work. The advanced Excel program allows you to create increasingly complex equations. If you've written your formula and configured your preset button, the app can do the math for you, saving you time and ensuring that you get correct results the first time.

8.8 It Has the Potential to Make Your Job Easier

You will be able to use Excel more quickly once you are more experienced with it. Microsoft Excel provides a range of keyboard shortcuts that can make you perform faster and develop more advanced Excel methods that you can use in the Microsoft Office suite. You'll now be able to view the data in Excel sheets from a variety of apps, reducing any need to re-enter data and improving workflow performance. The easier your work is to do, and the more trained you are, the more likely you are to enjoy it. Indeed, statistics indicate that cheerful workers are

20% more productive than their miserable counterparts. If the work is better, you will be a happy and productive employee.

8.9 How to Make Yourself a Valuable Employee at Work

Being a proactive participant helps you further your profession while still ensuring your work protection. It will make you become more important to the company if you were more successful, and better educated and experienced in your job activities. That's exactly what advanced Excel preparation can provide. Employees can constantly search for opportunities to increase their contribution to the company in order to prevent being substituted by new workers with more advanced skillsets. You must develop and master new techniques to stay ahead of the rankings and set yourself up for increased stability and development.

Advanced Excel skills and experience can help both your staff and your business in a variety of ways. It improves efficiency and output. Yes, as previously said, advanced Microsoft Excel preparation will improve employee performance and productivity, culminating in improved organizational efficiency and productivity. The more effective your employees are, the easier they can finish assignments and initiatives, enabling you to give greater support to your clients and associates while also delivering more work with less time. Even if advanced Excel preparation saves the employee a ½ hour per week, when multiplied by the number of workers in the organization or company, that will add up to a significant number of additional staff hours each week.

8.10 It relieves the IT support team of stress

When employees aren't well-versed in all aspects of a tech application, it's up to the IT department to pick up the slack. IT employees who go from workspace to workspace to train colleagues are unable to focus on more efficient activities such as device upgrades, security, and hardware installation and maintenance.

Moreover, just because the IT department can assist workers with technological usage, does not mean they are utilizing it to its maximum capacity and supplying the products with the requisite data and knowledge. Their abilities are more specialized, and they do not understand the meaning or significance of the details they are helping the employee with. Employees who are skilled in advanced Excel can lever their own data management, saving resources and producing superior outcomes than those who must depend on IT.

It can help you retain creativity and provide your staff a more enjoyable working experience.

Employees that are respected focus on learning new skills that would enable them to progress, not just in their current position but also up the corporate ladder. Your employees' work satisfaction will suffer if you don't feed their appetite to learn, and they will be less likely to pursue their career path in your business. As employees are trained, they become more valuable to the business, which boosts morale and gives the best employees an incentive to continue.

Employee training is crucial for advancing in the workforce, rising productivity, and retaining a healthy workforce. If you wish to engage in onsite preparation and hold your workers up to speed on advanced Excel processes, or provide them the freedom to pursue outside training opportunities, including a master's degree for Advanced Excel coursework, ongoing learning for your employees is vital to helping you grow your company and remain ahead of your industry's rivals.

As they say, awareness is an asset, and empowering staff to use vital services to their maximum capacity is the best way to encourage them, improve their talents, and maximize their contribution to the company. Using specialized Excel preparation to improve workers' daily jobs would keep them involved, progressing, and performing on time.

8.11 It allows you to make more use of an asset you already own

Your company's information programs are commodities, and they can be underutilized if employees aren't trained to make the best of them. Continued Excel preparation can help you get the best out of that asset, and other tools, such as inventory management systems, that aren't being utilized to their maximum extent. For example, you would improve inventory management and allow efficient utilization of your assets if your employees can correctly organize and streamline calculations.

It allows you to improve employee skills at low cost and with little effort. Workers in your business have always been educated with the initial Excel software, but implementing simple training plans to teach them how to use the technology correctly will be much less expensive than having to educate new workers with the organization's processes and procedures that have little prior knowledge in these sophisticated technologies. Furthermore, for employees who have already shown intermediate proficiency, advanced training may be easy, taking only a few weeks or less. Rather than paying for external training services for your staff, you can save costs by hiring an onsite teacher who can teach a large number of them all at once. At a reduced cost, it helps in a more educated and skilled population.

Conclusion

Microsoft Excel is database software for recording, manipulating, and storing numeric data. In Excel, the ribbon is used to access different commands. The options dialog window allows you to configure a variety of features, such as the ribbon, formulas, proofing, and saving.

Excel's main advantage is that it allows for speedy data input. MS Excel features a Ribbon interface, which is a collection of instructions that may be used to do particular tasks, as opposed to other data entering and analysis techniques. The ribbon is divided into tabs, each of which has a number of command groups and keys that go with it. You may quickly choose instructions and perform operations by tapping the appropriate tab.

Overall, Microsoft Excel assists you in manipulating, monitoring, and interpreting data, allowing you to make better choices and save time and money. Whether you're working on a business project or managing personal databases and finances, Microsoft Excel has the tools you need to get the job done. It's an ideal tool for making custom spreadsheets based on templates for corporate usage, data analysis, and multimedia data presentation.

Excel is commonly used for data organization and financial reporting. It is seen in both corporate functions and for businesses of all sizes. Excel is used for accountants, investment managers, consultants, and individuals in all aspects of financial careers to fulfil their everyday tasks. With the internet playing such an important role in our lives and businesses, it's only natural that the interests of many would win out. Staying up to date on new technology has been a full-time task as Microsoft platforms continue to grow. Microsoft Excel will continue to be the most popular framework for analyzing results, creating maps and presentations, and integrating with powerful software for digital dashboards and business intelligence workflows.

Businesses are increasingly turning to cloud storage for data connectivity and collaboration. You will see Microsoft Excel's future over the next few years advancing at a breakneck pace to have multi-user access to vast data for research, monitoring, and significant improvements in performance and productivity. Custom solutions are expected in today's dynamic market climate to retain a competitive advantage and maximize income. Microsoft Excel consulting firms are the most knowledgeable on current and new developments. Having a retained specialist consultant is critical to achieving maximum strength and efficiency skills required to excel in the twenty-first century.

Excel is often unavoidable in marketing, but with the tips mentioned above, it doesn't have to be so intimidating. Practice makes perfect, as they say. These formulae, shortcuts, and methods will become second nature the more you utilize them.

Made in the USA
Columbia, SC
15 December 2021